Contents

New words

burrow
(noun)

chick

desert

fat
(noun)

feather

fog

ice

leaf
(leaves)

mountain

nest

ocean

sand

HOW do animals live in bad weather?

Many animals live in places with good weather and lots of food.

But some animals live in places with very bad weather.

Polar bears live in cold places. They live in the **ice** and snow.

This camel lives in a hot place. There is not much water here.

Bison live in very cold places. This bison has snow on its hair.

LOOK!

Look at the pages.
What lives in the snow?

Do animals live in very hot places?

These animals live in hot **deserts**.

The **sand** is hot. The shovel-snouted lizard cannot put its feet on the sand for long!

tail

The Cape ground squirrel has a big tail. The squirrel uses its tail to stay cool.

The fennec fox has big ears. They keep the fox cool in hot weather.

 FIND OUT!

Use books or the internet to find out what else a fennec fox uses its big ears for.

How do animals find food and water in the desert?

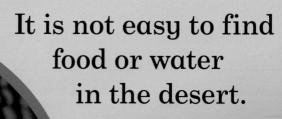

It is not easy to find food or water in the desert.

Sandgrouses travel a lot to find water for their **chicks**. They carry the water in their **feathers**.

Darkling beetles get water from **fog.**

Many desert animals stay in their **burrows** in the day because it is too hot.

They find food and water at night.

WATCH!

Watch the video (see page 32).
Why do the darkling beetles walk up the sand?

Why do camels have humps?

Camels do not eat or drink often.

They have **fat** in their humps.
Camels use this fat when
they cannot find food.

hump

The sand is not a problem for a camel's ears, eyes or nose.

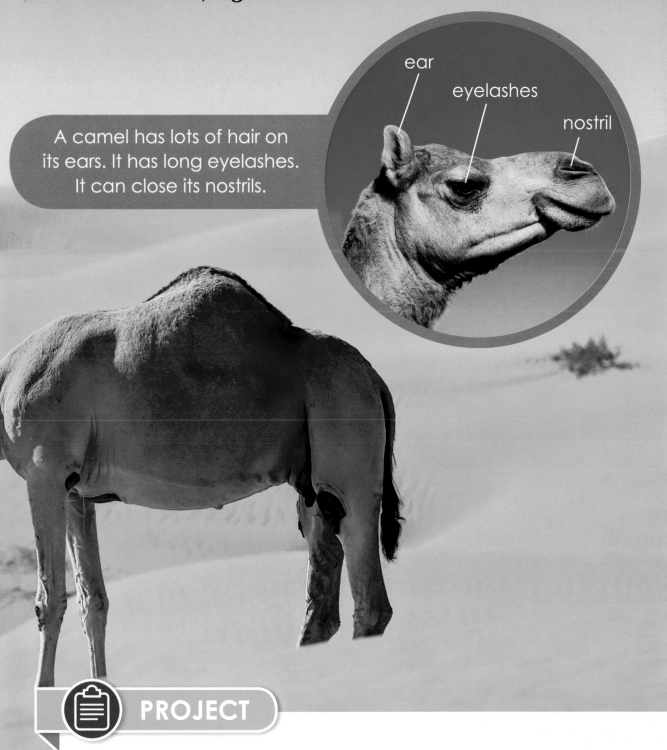

ear

eyelashes

nostril

A camel has lots of hair on its ears. It has long eyelashes. It can close its nostrils.

PROJECT

Work in a group.

Draw a picture of a camel. Label the different parts of its body. Explain how the camel lives in the hot, dry desert.

Why do tree frogs like rain?

These special tree frogs need rain for their babies.

The forest green tree frogs live in trees near water.

The mother tree frog makes a **nest** for her eggs.

A baby frog is a tadpole. The tadpoles come out of their eggs.

Rain changes the nest.

tadpole

Now, the tadpoles can go down to the water below and they can swim.

▶ WATCH!

Watch the video (see page 32).
What happens to the tadpoles after 20 days of rain?
What do the tadpoles eat?

Do animals live where there is no water?

In some places, there is no rain for months.

The water-holding frog lives under the ground when there is no water.

These chimpanzees live near a desert.

They walk for many kilometres to find water.

Sometimes there is no water in the river. These chimpanzees are trying to find water.

LOOK!

Look at the pages.
Where do the chimpanzees live?
What are the chimpanzees trying to find?

How do animals live in very cold places?

Winter is not easy for animals in cold places. The wind can be very cold.

Emperor penguins stay together to keep warm.

Different penguins stand on the outside of the group at different times. It is warmer in the middle.

A caribou has two coats of fur. The fur makes it warm.

fur

Arctic ground squirrels stay under the snow and sleep. They do not wake up for many months!

📖 **FIND OUT!**

Use books or the internet to find out why the emperor penguin's body is good for cold weather.

What do animals do before winter?

Some animals work hard before winter.

Pikas must find food and keep it safe for winter.

Sometimes they take food from other pikas' burrows.

Siberian chipmunks put **leaves** in their burrows. They want warm homes for winter.

The chipmunks find acorns for food and put them in their burrows.

acorn

Chipmunks need lots of acorns for the long winter.

▶ WATCH!

Watch the video (see page 32).
Where do the chipmunks live?
How many acorns does a chipmunk need for winter?

HOW do animals find food in the snow?

Animals in cold places need to find food.

Red foxes listen for small animals under the snow. They jump into the snow to catch them.

There is grass under this snow. Bison can find the grass with their heads.

Sika deer find plants and grass with their feet.

 THINK!

How would you try to find something under the snow?

23

HOW does a snow leopard live in the mountains?

It is often very cold in the mountains.

This snow leopard is not cold because it has long, thick fur.

The snow leopard's long tail helps it, too. The snow leopard puts its tail on its body when it sits or sleeps.

PROJECT

Work in a group.
Use books or the internet to find information about a snow leopard and a leopard.
How are they the same? How are they different?
Make a chart.

Why do some animals travel a long way?

Many animals travel to find good weather.

Some birds travel to warm places in winter.
There is more food in warm places.

Wildebeests travel to find rain. They want to eat new grass

The grey whale travels to the cold **ocean** to find food. It travels to the warm ocean to have babies.

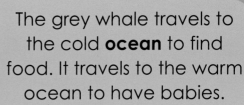

FIND OUT!

The Arctic tern travels further each year than any other animal. **Use books or the internet** to find out where it goes and how far it travels.

How can weather be a problem for animals?

The weather is changing everywhere.
This is a problem for animals.
It changes their homes.

When there is no rain, it's not
easy to find food and water.

The polar bears' home is too warm now. This is a problem.

Polar bears need cold weather because they need sea ice.

Polar bears walk on the sea ice and they find animals to eat.

THINK!

Why do polar bears need sea ice?
Where is their food?

Quiz

Choose the correct answers.

1 In a desert there is . . .
a no water.
b very little water.
c lots of water.

2 The fennec fox lives in . . .
a hot deserts.
b cold deserts.
c the snow and ice.

3 In the hot desert, many animals look for food and water . . .
a in the morning.
b at night.
c in the afternoon.

4 What is in a camel's hump?
a water
b sand
c fat

5 Chimpanzees walk for many kilometres . . .
   a to find deserts.
   b to find friends.
   c to find water.

6 When it is very cold and windy,
   emperor penguins . . .
   a jump in the sea.
   b sleep under the snow.
   c stand together.

7 Sika deer find food under the snow with . . .
   a their fingers.
   b their feet.
   c their ears.

8 Polar bears walk on sea ice to find . . .
   a food.
   b a home.
   c a family.

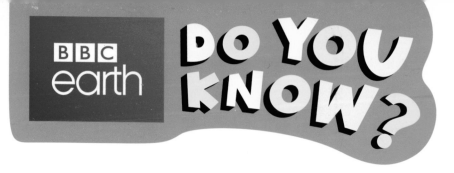

BBC earth — DO YOU KNOW?

Visit **www.ladybirdeducation.co.uk** for
FREE DO YOU KNOW? teaching resources.

- video clips with simplified voiceover and subtitles
- video and comprehension activities
- class projects and lesson plans
- audio recording of every book
- digital version of every book
- full answer keys

To access video clips, audio tracks and digital books:

1 Go to **www.ladybirdeducation.co.uk**
2 Click "Unlock book"
3 Enter the code below

DSoewidcxn

Stay safe online! Some of the **DO YOU KNOW?** activities ask children to do extra research online. Remember:

- ensure an adult is supervising;
- use established search engines such as Google or Kiddle;
- children should never share personal details, such as name, home or school address, telephone number or photos.